An Nasihah

Islamic Curriculum

المنهج الاسلامي للأطفال

Workbook
4

- Fiqh
- Aḥādīth
- Sīrah
- Tārīkh
- `Aqā'id
- Akhlāq
- Ādāb

5th edition June 2019

British Library Cataloguing in Publication Data. A catalogue record for this book is available from the British Library.

Every effort has been made to ensure the correctness of the content. The publishers will gladly receive information enabling them to rectify any error or omission in subsequent editions.

An Nasihah Publications Ltd.
114 Harborough Road
Leicester LE2 4LD
United Kingdom
www.an-nasihah.com
admin@an-nasihah.com

Distributor in the UK
Azhar Academy, London
020 8911 9797
www.azharacademy.com
sales@azharacademy.com

Distributors in Australia
Melbourne, Victoria
Mufti Zeeyad Ravat
0499 559 199
zravat@hotmail.com

Distributor in Canada
Mawlana Zakariyya Desai
647-781-7313
nasihahcanada@gmail.com

Perth, Western Australia
Shaykh Burhaan Mehtar
0452 217 866
iqraacademyperth@gmail.com

Printed by Imak Offset in Turkey

Name: _____

Class: _____

اَلْحَمْدُ لِلّٰهِ رَبِّ الْعَالَمِيْنَ
وَالصَّلَاةُ وَالسَّلَامُ عَلٰى نَبِيِّنَا مُحَمَّدٍ
وَعَلٰى اٰلِهِ وَصَحْبِهِ أَجْمَعِيْنَ

بِسْمِ اللّٰهِ الرَّحْمٰنِ الرَّحِيْمِ

Contents

Fiqh	**6**
Aḥādīth	**22**
Sīrah	**44**
Tārīkh	**66**
`Aqā'id	**78**
Akhlāq	**108**
Ādāb	**124**

Fiqh

فقه

Khuffayn

What is masaḥ ‘alal khuffayn?

_____

_____

_____

_____

_____

_____

_____

Khuffayn

Working with a partner, complete the spider diagram below with a summary of the conditions for the khuff.

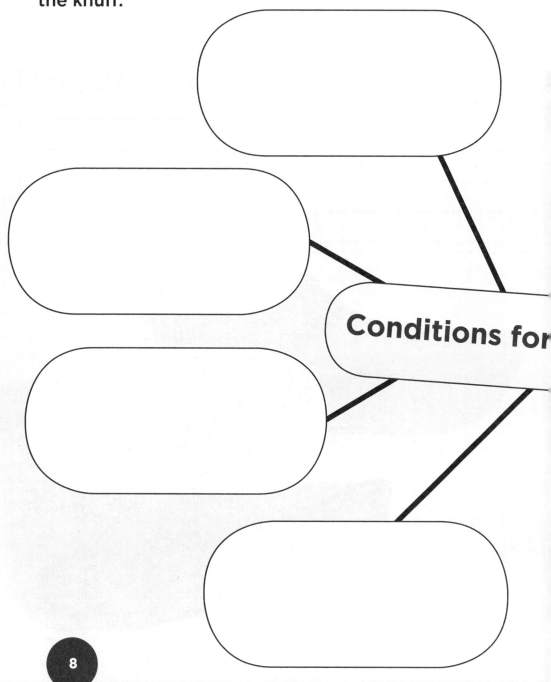

Conditions for

Khuffayn

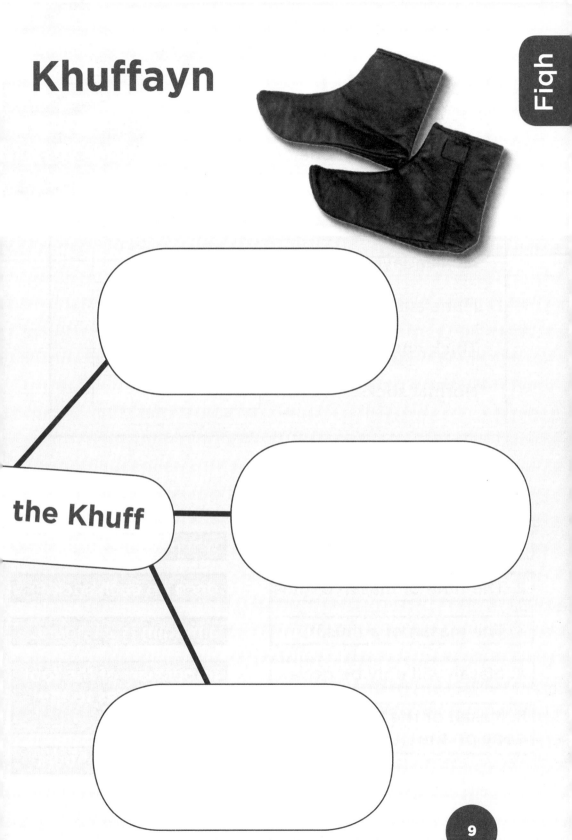

the Khuff

Khuffayn

Write next to each one of the following words whether it is permissible to do masaḥ on them or not.

Mujalladayn

Muna'alayn

Thick non-leather socks

Normal socks

Match the following sentences:

1. The duration of masaḥ for	when wuḍū' breaks
2. The time of masaḥ begins	once on each sock
3. The masaḥ of a musāfir	a muqīm is 24 hours
4. Masaḥ will only be done	upper part of the foot from the toes to the foreleg
5. Masaḥ of the khuff will be done on the	will last for 72 hours

Khuffayn

What are the three things that break the masaḥ?

1.

2.

3.

Masaḥ on wounds

Fill in the boxes below.

Masaḥ allowed

Masaḥ not allowed

Wājib acts of Ṣalāh

Fill in the blanks:

three - every - nafl - tashahhud - rak'āt - first
qaumah - two - recite - sunnah - after - sajdah
six - farḍ - fātiḥah - finish - qunūt - calmly

1. In the first _____ rak'ah of farḍ ṣalāh, it is wājib to _____ Qur'ān.

2. Every time you perform a sunnah or _____ ṣalāh, you have to read Sūrah _____ in every rak'ah.

3. In _____ ṣalāh, you must read Sūrah Fātiḥah in the _____ two rak'ah.

4. In farḍ ṣalāh, _____ Sūrah Fātiḥah, you must also read at least _____ small āyāt in the first two rak'ah.

5. It is wājib to also read at least three small āyāt in _____ rak'ah of wājib, _____ and nafl ṣalāh.

6. You must stand up straight after doing rukū'. This is called _____.

Wājib acts of Ṣalāh

7. After doing one _____, you must sit up before doing another sajdah. This is called jalsah.

8. It is wājib to do everything _____ and properly. To rush and not do the actions of ṣalāh properly is sinful.

9. After every 2 _____, you must sit after both sajdahs.

10. Whenever you sit after 2 rak'ah, you have to read _____.

11. Every time you want to _____ your ṣalāh, you must do so by saying salām.

12. In Witr Ṣalāh, it is wājib to recite _____ and to say the takbīr for it.

13. In Ṣalātul 'īd you must say _____ extra takbīrs.

Sajdah as-Sahw

When does Sajdah as-Sahw become necessary?

_____
_____
_____
_____
_____
_____

What are the steps of performing Sajdah as-Sahw? Explain it in four sentences.

1: _____

2: _____

3: _____

4: _____

Ṣawm

Types of Fasts

Breaking of the Fast

Match the following sentences by putting the correct number in front of the second part.

| 1. Qaḍā' means to |
| 2. The Kaffārah of fasting is |
| 3. Kaffārah is a penalty which has to be given |
| 4. If one cannot fast 60 days continuously then they could |

	when you do something that is forbidden during a fast.
	feed 60 poor people two full meals
	do an action again.
	to fast for 60 days continuously

Breaking of the Fast

Make a mnemonic to remember the actions that make only qaḍā' wājib.

1: _____ _____

2: _____ _____

3: _____ _____

4: _____ _____

5: _____ _____

6: _____ _____

Write down three things that don't break your fast.

1: _____

2: _____

3: _____

Ṣawm

Fill in the blanks:

Terminal - Fidyah - Traveller - Qaḍā'
ill - Worse - Travelling - Ṣadaqah al-Fiṭr
Hungry - Excused

There are a few types of people who have been _____ from fasting if they are in a certain condition. A person who is ill or extremely _____ and thinks that the illness will get _____ or that they will die, then they will not need to fast. Similarly if a person is _____, then they will also not be required to fast. However in all of the above cases, if a person is no longer _____, hungry or a _____, they will need to do _____ of the missed fasts. If a person is suffering a _____ illness then they can give _____ for each missed fast. If they come out of that illness, they will also need to make qaḍā'. The value of fidyah is the same as _____.

Ṣawm (Fidyah)

Colour in the picture below and find out the value of Ṣadaqah al-Fiṭr. Write it down on the bedside table below.

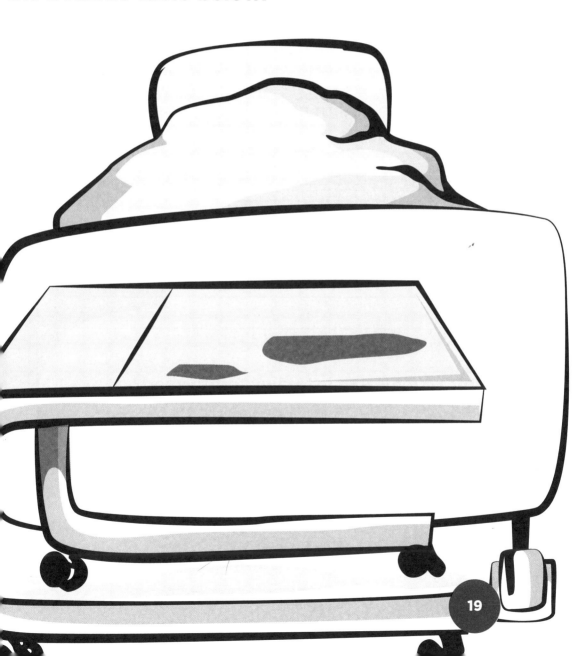

Tarāwīḥ

Add the numbers below. Write the answer in the box using bubble writing

4 + 6 + 8 + 2

Copy out the ḥadīth about tarāwīḥ ṣalāh from your coursebook.

_____

_____

_____

_____

_____

After which ṣalāh is tarāwīḥ performed?

_____

Tarāwīḥ

Mention five things that you have learnt about tarāwīḥ.

Aḥādīth

احاديث

Colour in the word ḥadīth.

Complete the word by joining the dots.

Feeding Others

Can you guide Ilyās to the poor family's house so that he could give them something to eat?

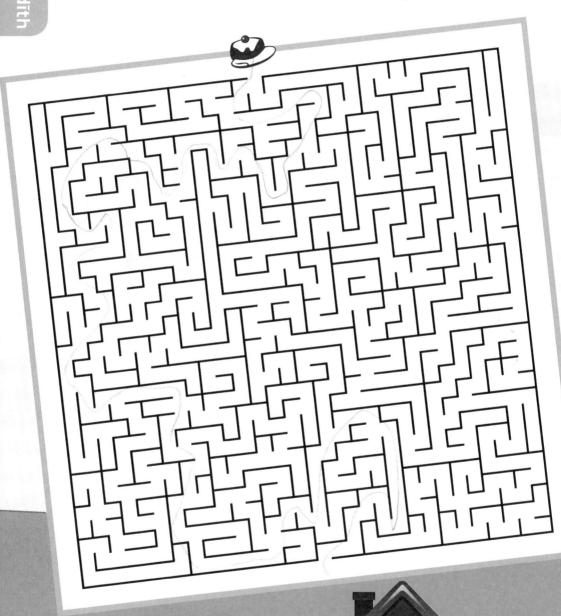

Feeding Others

Find the words below in this word search.

```
N H W C H G H X Y N U F Q T C
F R P W H U H V J E N Y K J F
U H X P N A B O R Y W B D O I
Y C A G E X R U K F K B Q R Z
Z T R I N W T I X T T F X W B
U Y I I K A M P T T W E C Y L
U L X M E U K U P Y X E R D H
H Q D R A K R O S P D D B E X
J A C O B L A M I N A I K E U
H Z U H O V A N V J M N J D Q
N H N L H F S C U T M G O N L
M S A D A Q A H K I A H N V Q
Z Y O S A D F M A M H H T W H
A O P P V D C T O N U J X Q B
V U P Q Z W W N K Q M V H S E
```

ANIMAL
CALAMITY
CHARITY
CREATURE
DEED
FEEDING
FOOD
HUNGRY
MUḤAMMAD
SADAQAH

No to Racism

Translate the following ḥadīth into English and colour the hands using different colours.

اِنَّكَ لَسْتَ بِخَيْرٍ مِّنْ اَحْمَرَ وَلَا اَسْوَدَ اِلَّا اَنْ تَفْضُلَهُ بِتَقْوٰى

You are neither _better_ **than a** _black_ **person or a red person unless you surpass him in** _piety_ **.**

26

No to Racism

Match the following sentences by putting the correct number in front of the second part.

1. Every single person is part of the creation of Allāh سبحانه وتعالى

2. The only thing that can make a person better

3. Allāh does not look at your forms or your bodies

4. The first Mu'adhin was Bilāl رضي الله عنه

[ ] than another is good deeds and piety

[ ] who was a black person from Abyssinia

[ ] and they are all equal in the eyes of Allāh سبحانه وتعالى

[ ] but he looks at your heart and your actions

Good Character

Write down a few good manners you can think of.

Help parents.

Do good Aqalaq.

Do good Adab

Do good Manners.

listen that your every thing parents say

28

Good Character

Now write down a few bad manners you can think of.

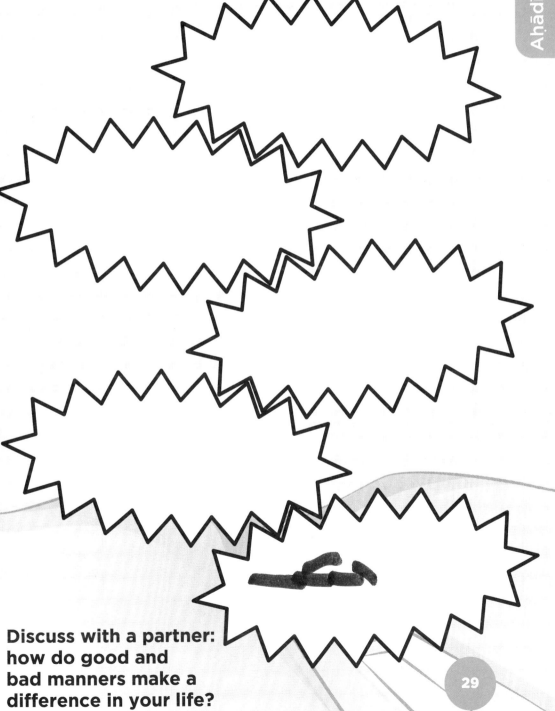

Discuss with a partner: how do good and bad manners make a difference in your life?

Good Character

Find the words below in this word search

```
M O H U F H J B D Q H R L S T Q U X
Z I Z V Q K Z G F H O O W N B L B T
E X L M H P X Z T L K C X P K R K N
N X H S N W E W E Y L I F X L X C O
Y S A B U Y K F T D F X S E Q W S M
C P O W J M R R U A T R D U P I V S
L E I C K I N D Y Y J O I J H M H E
H Q S R X V I L X A M H L C N X S K
N M O N H Q T F R O E N D C H K M D
U M B I R Q P B W L B D W E M V S D
E L P O E P J N P G A E F K A Q X A
Y M I F F H I F G N I V D I N K O I
Q L A K C D U R M I J J F I N H W G
R V O N B L I O K R B P E L E J Q H
S A L R I B C Y D A G B L O R N N P
W O Z C S H B I W C W N J Q S Z T O
B N H W L P O V F J B D F S G Z O O
P J Q U M A C O A H W Z Y D U X C R
```

CARING	HELPFUL
KIND	MANNERS
MODEL	MUSLIM
OBEDIENT	PEOPLE
POOR	RICH
ROLE	

Thanking Others

'Ārifah just gave you one sweet from her pocket.
What should you say to her?

Make a list of the things that people do for you each
day and remember to thank them each time.

Example: My mum looks after me.

_____

_____

_____

_____

_____

_____

Friends

Colour in the following ḥadīth.

اَلْمَرْءُ مَعَ مَنْ أَحَبَّ

A person will be with whom he
laxes .

Think about all the good qualities that you should look for when making friends and write 5 of them down below.

1._____

2._____

3._____

4._____

5._____

Friends

There are many bad qualities that you should stay away from and also stay away from people who have them.

Unscramble the following bad qualities and then find them in the word search.

Linyg
Snaetlig
Blliyung
Sarienwg
Derecipsst
Ietnpmait
Fisoloh
Lzay
Mlsirey
Rdue
Ssieflh
Geredy
Cerul

```
F H U M D G Y S B G
O S N C I N D M U N
O I T F S I E P L I
L F I U R L E Y L R
I L D S E A R Z Y A
S E Y S S E G A I E
H S O Y P T Z L N W
O Y L R E S I M G S
L E U R C L Y I N G
T N E I T A P M I H
```

Kindness

Can you help little 'Afīfah take her treasure box of kindness and love safely to the centre of the maze?

Kindness

Write down three ways in which we can be kind to others.

1.

_____

2.

_____

3.

_____

Write down how you felt when someone was kind to you.

_____

_____

_____

Trust

Colour in the following words and write down what trust means to you.

The Trusted One

_____

_____

_____

_____

Keys to Paradise

Make a colourful poster of the words
لَا إِلٰهَ إِلَّا اللّٰهُ and include the translation of
the ḥadīth.

Dhikr

Complete the following translation:

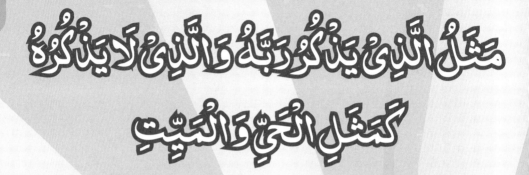

He who _____ his Lord and he who doesn't are like the _____ and the dead.

Use this table to keep track of your weekly dhikr.

Day	Type of dhikr	Amount

Dhikr

Write down some dhikr in Arabic or English in the bubbles below:

ALHAMDU LILLAH

SUBHANALLAH

Du'ā'

Allāh سبحانه وتعالى loves to give us all that we ask for. What will you ask Allāh سبحانه وتعالى for? Write it down in the boxes below.

Du'ā'

Allāh سبحانه وتعالى has control over all the treasures of the heavens and the earth and He can give whatever he wants to anyone who asks.

Colour in the picture below and write down some of the treasures of Allāh سبحانه وتعالى you can think of.

43

Sīrah

سيرة النبي ﷺ

The Pledge Of 'Aqabah

1. In which year of prophethood did the pledge of 'Aqabah take place?

_____

_____

2. How many people came to take the pledge with the Prophet ﷺ?

_____

_____

3. Where had the people come from?

_____

_____

4. What did they pledge to do?

_____

_____

The Pledge Of 'Aqabah

5. Why is this pledge know as the Pledge of 'Aqabah?

_____

_____

6. Who did the Prophet ﷺ send to teach them?

_____

_____

7. What did he do after being sent as a teacher?

_____

_____

8. What was the result of his teaching in Madīnah?

_____

_____

The Pledge Of 'Aqabah

Unscramble the following words and find them in the word search below.

Pegedl

Mmhaaumd

Aabhqa

Mīaadnh

Aāhll

Yrtabhi

Tcheear

Tīwdah

```
T  U  P  Z  V  H  E  D  Y  S
A  J  Y  F  G  G  A  Z  Q  R
W  F  W  T  D  M  Q  L  P  X
H  L  H  E  M  T  A  B  L  T
I  T  L  A  R  I  B  I  K  A
D  P  H  C  N  O  A  R  Y  M
A  U  T  H  K  I  H  H  C  S
M  N  X  E  K  K  D  T  Q  K
U  A  T  R  F  G  E  A  V  R
W  Q  X  C  T  R  Z  Y  M  V
```

The Pledge Of 'Aqabah

Islām guides us to keep our promises at all times. Choose one good thing you can promise to do over the next week and see if you can stick to it without leaving it out.

1. Tasbīḥ after ṣalāh
2. Washing the dishes after eating
3. Reading the Mu'awwidhatayn before sleeping
4. Reciting the sleeping and waking up du'ā'
5. Helping a different person each day

Day	I did it	I couldn't
Example	✓	x
Monday		
Tuesday		
Wednesday		
Thursday		
Friday		
Saturday		
Sunday		

The Pledge Of 'Aqabah

Draw a picture about the Pledge of 'Aqabah and the different things that may have been there. Remember to include the following:

- A Hill
- Night sky
- Some of the points of the pledge

Hijrah

Find the words below in the word search.

M	J	N	O	X	L	E	B	F	S	G
B	I	A	M	S	A	A	E	R	N	Y
X	A	H	L	M	K	P	V	C	O	P
V	F	N	S	R	H	P	I	Y	I	R
K	X	D	I	A	L	Z	L	R	S	E
Z	L	A	Z	O	H	A	L	E	S	D
Z	S	Q	T	R	J	E	H	V	E	I
Q	R	T	O	E	T	M	A	E	S	P
N	E	B	E	A	N	Q	Y	N	S	S
D	N	Z	R	W	P	R	S	G	O	F
A	T	G	R	E	O	Z	A	E	P	D
L	I	T	H	A	U	R	O	G	R	W
M	Q	U	R	A	Y	S	H	A	E	L
H	A	Q	A	R	U	S	W	I	P	D
A	Y	X	J	K	T	E	P	Z	L	T
O	Y	A	U	L	R	U	P	G	Q	A
J	V	U	S	F	A	B	C	D	F	R
R	X	M	H	V	V	A	C	U	O	G
C	B	A	M	Z	V	U	E	E	S	W
X	D	O	P	I	H	Y	W	G	Q	E

Migrate   Quraysh   Enraged
Bani Hashim   Revenge   Plotted
Evil   Ali   Possessions
Abū Bakr   Thaur   Spider
Asma   Reward   Surāqah

Hijrah

Using the pictures below, re-tell the events during Hijrah in your own words.

Event 1 - Migration

_____

_____

_____

_____

Event 2 – Evil Plot

_____

_____

_____

_____

Event 3 – Allāh's Protection

_____

_____

_____

_____

Arrival in Madīnah

Imagine you arrived at a new place just like Qubā. Your job is to design a new masjid, use labels to describe the different parts both inside and outside of the masjid. Also give your masjid a name.

Arrival in Madīnah

When the Prophet ﷺ and Abū Bakr رضي الله عنه arrived in Madīnah, the city was filled with joy. Write a 7 line rhyming poem describing how the people may have felt.

The Masjid in Madīnah

Design the masjid of Madīnah using plasticine and read the coursebook chapter 'The Masjid of Madīnah'.

In the box below draw the masjid of Madīnah. Remember to draw the things that the actual masjid was made of.

Islamic Brotherhood

Split the class into groups. In each group there should be an even amount of Muhājirs and Anṣārīs.

Select a spokesperson who relates what is happening.

Each of the Anṣār to be paired with a Muhājir.

Anṣār to act out their daily routines and care and treat the Muhājir like they would their own brother or sister.

Treaties with the Jews

How many tribes did Madīnah have and what were the names of the tribes?

_____

_____

_____

_____

Circle the correct letter, T (True) or F (False).

1. The Jews had to revert to Islām whilst living amongst the Muslims.　　T　F

2. Each group would help the other if it was to come under attack by an outside aggressor.　　T　F

3. They would treat each other with respect and show kindness to all.　　T　F

4. It was also agreed that in any dispute, the Prophet's decision would be final.　　T　F

5. All three of the tribes were party to the pact.　　T　F

The Hypocrites

How would you describe a hypocrite?

_____

_____

_____

_____

HYPOCRITE

Qualities of a hypocrite...

_____

_____

_____

The Battles

Fill in the blanks

The _____ were infuriated that the Prophet and his Ṣaḥābah were _____ to escape to _____ and _____ themselves safely. The Muslims left behind in _____ were mercilessly _____.

On seeing the power of the Muslims _____, the Quraysh decided to _____ the _____ and be done with them once and for all. For this reason the Quraysh _____ on all Makkans. The _____ gathered was then _____ in trade and the _____ were then used to fund a _____ against the _____.

The Battle of Badr

Create a word search and ask your friend to complete it. Write your words in the box below.

The Battle of Uḥud

Make your own crossword using the words and definitions below.

1. Revenge - To inflict hurt or harm on someone for an injury on oneself or another.

2. Launch - To start an activity.

3. Hypocrite - A person who pretends to put on a false appearance of virtue or religion.

4. Hill - A naturally raised area of land.

5. Prophet - Someone who brings a message from Allāh.

6. Protected - Keep safe from harm or injury.

7. Defiant - Someone who keeps trying.

8. Mutilated - Causing serious damage to the body.

9. Freedom - The right to act, speak or think as one wants.

The Jewish Tribes

Write a short article retelling the story in your own words about the arrival of the Messenger ﷺ in Madīnah and the issues he had to deal with in the blessed city.

The Jewish Tribes

Find the letters below and unscramble them to make a word.

342h23a45n65d865m43a2i543

Madinah

Write a few sentences about the word you have found.

_____

_____

_____

_____

_____

_____

Battle of Aḥzāb Dhul Qa'dah 5 AH

Imagine you are a news reporter present at the time of The Battle of Aḥzāb. Use the space provided to write a short article of what you see.

Tārīkh

تاريخ

66

Yūsuf عليه السلام

Read the text in the coursebook and answer the following questions.

Who was Ibrāhīm عليه السلام?

_____

Who was Isḥāq عليه السلام?

_____

Who was Ya'qūb عليه السلام?

_____

Why do we not attribute anyone as a partner to Allāh سبحانه وتعالى?

_____

What were the names of the two fellow prisoners and what were they asked to do?

_____

Why did Yūsuf عليه السلام stay in prison for some years?

_____

_____

Yūsuf عليه السلام

Draw a picture of a well and write how this picture is linked with the story of Yūsuf عليه السلام.

Yūsuf عليه السلام

Unscramble the words and write them in the blank spaces.

rseestuhoo

otsneh

eamrd

orsipn

midwos

neevs

soptneuel

agniudra

live

udjelbm

srutt

Yūsuf عليه السلام

Match up the sentences

He rushed to the prison and asked Yūsuf عليه السلام

Yūsuf عليه السلام not only gave the meaning

He said, "You shall sow seven years as usual,

Then after that will come seven hard years

Finally, a year will come when the people will have

The king was so touched by

Yūsuf عليه السلام asked that the king

Zalīkha was called and she admitted saying,

Yūsuf's عليه السلام innocence was now known

The people that were in charge of these storehouses

They would steal a lot of the food and

When Rayyan, the king, spoke to Yūsuf عليه السلام,

Yūsuf عليه السلام was an honest man

Yūsuf

but explained the solution too.

the meaning of this dream.

plenty of crops and when they will press (wine and oil).''

the wisdom of Yūsuf عليه السلام that he wanted to meet him.

which will devour all that you have prepared for them, save a little of that which you have stored.

check the case first.

"We know no evil of him"

he told him that he was trusted in his royal court

to all the people.

were not honest.

not distribute it to the people equally.

he did not like to see people doing wrong things

and that which you harvest, leave it except for a little which you need to eat.

Yūsuf عليه السلام

1. Write down adjectives (describing words) about how you would feel if you were all alone in the wilderness.

_____   _____   _____

_____   _____   _____

2. Can you find your way through the wilderness?

YOU

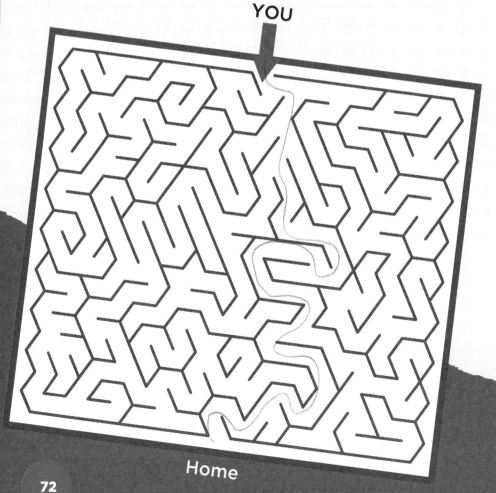

Home

Yūsuf عليه السلام

"O camel-riders! You are surely _____!"
They said, coming towards them, "What is it
you have _____?"

They said, "We have lost the king's _____,
and he who brings it shall have a _____
load as a reward. The brothers answered,
"By Allāh, you know we have not come to do
_____ in the land, and are not thieves."

Yūsuf عليه السلام's officers asked, "And what shall
be the _____ for it, if you are proven as
liars?" They said, "The _____ shall be that
in whoever's _____ the cup is found that
person will be taken as a _____.

Yūsuf عليه السلام began the _____. He searched
all their bags, leaving young Binyāmīn's until
_____. The king's goblet was, of course,
found in Binyāmīn's bag.

Yūsuf عليه السلام

Read the two paragraphs below carefully. Incorrect words have been placed intentionally. Find those words and put a line through them and write the correct word near it.

The brothers did [_____] know how to face their uncle [_____]. Were they going to make him dinner [_____] again like they did for Yūsuf عليه السلام?

The heaviest [_____] brother said he can [_____] go back and so he too remained in Yemen [_____].

Ya'qub عليه السلام was put to the test again. He was very angry [_____]. He told his daughters [_____],

"Go, O my sons, and find out about Yūsuf and his brother, and despair not of the mercy of Allāh سبحانه وتعالى. No one despairs of the mercy of Allāh except the unbelievers."

They came to Yemen [_____] in front of Yūsuf عليه السلام and put forward their condition shouting [_____]:

"O ruler! Misfortune has touched us and our neighbours , and we bring but rich [_____] [_____] merchandise, so fill for us the measure and

Yūsuf عليه السلام

be charitable unto our cousins [   ].
Allāh سبحانه وتعالى will help [   ] the charitable."

This was not [   ] much to bear for Yūsuf عليه السلام. How long will the story [   ] be kept? How long will he see his neighbours [   ] suffer? He said to them, "Do you know what you did to Yūsuf and his brother when you were not aware?" The brothers were proud [   ]! No one except them knew of this secret. Could this be their very uncle [   ] whom they had plotted to hide [   ] all those years ago?

They said in absolute delight [   ], "Are you Aḥmad [   ]?" Yūsuf عليه السلام said, "I am Yūsuf and this is my brother (pointing at Binyamin)."

Yūsuf عليه السلام

Summarise the story of Yūsuf عليه السلام below.

_____

_____

_____

_____

_____

_____

_____

_____

_____

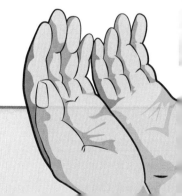

Yūsuf عليه السلام

After reading the story of Yūsuf عليه السلام think of all the lessons that you have learnt. Write down as many as you can. Compare your lessons with a partner.

_____

_____

_____

_____

_____

_____

_____

ʻAqāʼid

عقائد

Major Signs

Find the words below in the word search:

```
J L J C X J E C S D N I W O A V
E L U N K G E F F O A Q M C E S
S E W F B Z H W I M P U S H Q F
V S M O K E S T A R N R E J F N
M W V A S A C W B L E T D C I O
P H F T J U X N Z V E U E I Z J
V I K T R U M P E T T U L K C B
A X J T I G J I F G H Y L U R D
F R S U S M L A D E R Z B J N Z
Y E K V H E R N Y H L E C G V I
D S A V B P W D U J A W M C U C
C A R Q H O A L M S I M D E C R
L W J W P E M V T S J N E T D T
F M P J S H M G E Z M E X T V S
V N B K A B A H L J X B F Z J A
Q A R C P L T U A H T V Z G L I
```

YA'JŪJ   BEAST   BELIEVERS
DAJJĀL   WIND   EMERGENCE
FIRE   WEST   MAHDĪ
MA'JŪJ   SMOKE   SUN
TRUMPET

Major Signs

Look at the 'Major Signs of Qiyāmah' and write them out below using fancy handwriting.

The Mahdī

Complete the following sentences:

Mahdī means _____

The Mahdī will be a man _____

The Mahdī will appear from the descendants of

_____

The Mahdī will follow and rule according _____

The people will take allegiance to him _____

His name will be _____ and

his father's name _____

The Dajjāl

On a piece of A4 paper, design a poster showing the facts about Dajjāl.

Who was Tamīm ad-Dāri رضي الله عنه?

_____

The Dajjāl

Look at the pictures below. Write a caption next to the picture to explain what is happening. Relate it back to pages in the coursebook.

The Dajjāl

Answer the following:

What was found in Balsān?

_____

What was found in Tiberias?

_____

What was found in Zugara?

_____

How did the Prophet treat the Arabs who fought him?

_____

Who was the person that was asking the questions?

_____

When it is time for him to come out, what will he do?

_____

What is Ṭaibah referring to?

_____

What will prevent the Dajjāl from entering Madīnah?

_____

The Dajjāl

"Behold, he is in the Syrian sea or sea of Yemen; no, rather he is from the eastern direction. He then pointed with his hand towards the East." (Ṣaḥīḥ Muslim)

Fill in the compass directions and colour it in.

The Dajjāl

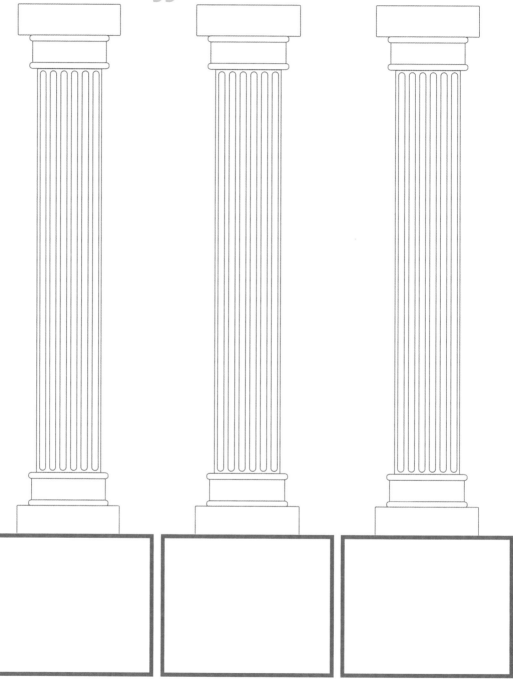

The Dajjāl

In the pillars, state 3 different ways in which you can be protected against Dajjāl. Try to include relevant information and colour the pillars in.

Try to memorise one āyāh from Sūrah al-Kahf each week.

Complete the dot-to-dot picture below.

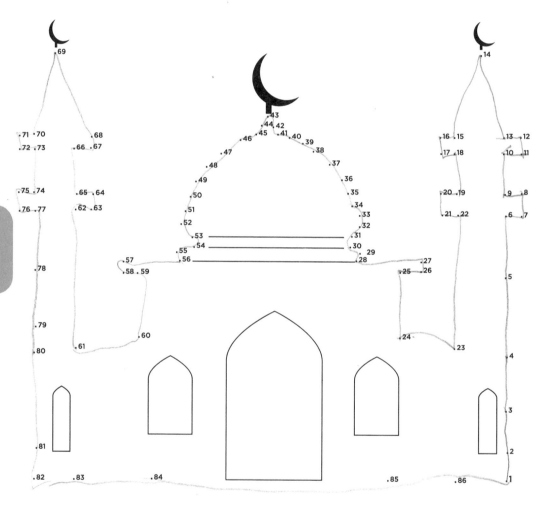

'Aqā'id

The Dajjāl

Colour in the masjid below

Ya'jūj & Ma'jūj

Study the Braille alphabet below.

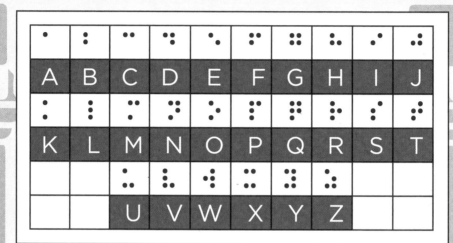

Write down what has been said:

When ___YAJUJ and majug are let___
___loose they rush___
_____

Ya'jūj & Ma'jūj

⠶⠶⠐⠇⠶⠶ ⠶⠶ ⠶⠶⠶⠶ ⠶⠶
⠶⠶⠶⠶⠶⠶⠶⠶

⠶⠶ ⠶⠶⠶⠶ ⠶⠶⠶ ⠶⠶⠶ ⠂
⠶⠶⠶⠶⠶ ⠶⠶ ⠶⠶⠶⠶⠶ ⠶⠶⠶

'Aqā'id

91

'Īsā عليه السلام

Think of a name for a penpal. Your penpal is not a Muslim and has asked you to explain about what 'Īsā عليه السلام role will be when the end of the world comes near.

Using the information in your course book, write a letter to your penpal explaining in your own words what will happen when 'Isā عليه السلام returns to the world..

'Īsā  عليه السلام

Create a poster highlighting our beliefs with regard to 'Īsā عليه السلام.

Major Signs

Fill in the blanks

Allāh will send _____ upon 'Isā علیه السلام that "Such a _____ of mine is now going to _____ that no power will be able to stop them. Therefore take my _____ and ascend the Mount of _____." Then Ya'jūj & Ma'jūj will emerge and _____ forth in all their fury.

When those from among them who constitute the former part of their _____ pass the lake of _____ (which is in northern Palestine), they will drink up all the _____ of that lake and by the time those that are at the back of the same army pass the lake, they will say, "There used to be water here (long ago).

When they reach the Mount of _____ in Jerusalem, they will _____ proclaim: "We have _____ the people of the earth, now we will destroy those in the _____." So saying this they will fire their _____ towards the sky, when the arrows return to the _____ they will be _____ stained.

In the meantime, 'Isā علیه السلام will be on the Mount of Ṭūr with the _____. 'Isā علیه السلام and the _____ will make Du'ā' to Allāh سبحانه وتعالى (to remove this

_____). As a result, Allāh سبحانه وتعالى will cause
_____ to appear on the _____ of each
and every _____ of these people which will
cause their _____ suddenly. When 'Isā عليه السلام
and the Muslims _____ from Mount Ṭūr there
will _____ be a single space on the land where
the dead _____ bodies of these people is not
_____ , giving off a bad _____ .

'Isā عليه السلام and the Muslims will once more
_____ unto Allāh سبحانه وتعالى as a result of
which Allāh سبحانه وتعالى will _____ down huge
_____ whose necks will be as _____ as
that of the necks of _____ , and they will dump
these_____ in a place where Allāh سبحانه وتعالى wills.
Allāh سبحانه وتعالى will then send down heavy _____ ;
the waters of which will _____ in every part of
the earth _____ it thoroughly. It will rain for a
period of _____ days.

Allāh سبحانه وتعالى will order the _____ to yield
forth its _____ in abundance. There will
be such _____ and prosperity that one
_____ will be sufficient for a whole group,
while the _____ thereof will suffice to cast a
_____ over them. The milk of one _____
will be sufficient for many _____ while one

Major Signs

milk giving _____ will be sufficient for a whole _____. One milk giving goat will be _____ for a whole family.

Sayyidinā Abū Hurairah رضي الله عنه narrates that every day Ya'jūj and _____ break (dig) through the _____ erected by _____ until they reach the _____ of it to that extent that they can actually see the _____ on the other side. They then _____ (home) saying that "We will _____ through tomorrow." But Allāh سبحانه وتعالى causes the _____ to revert to its _____ thickness and the next day they start _____ through the wall all over _____, this process continues each day _____ as long as Allāh سبحانه وتعالى wills them to remain _____ . When Allāh سبحانه وتعالى wishes them to be_____, at the end of that day they will say, "If _____ wills, tomorrow we will break through." The _____ day they will find the wall as they had _____ it the previous day (i.e. it will not have _____ to its _____ state) and after _____ the remaining part of it they will _____." (Aḥmad, Tirmiḍi, Ibn Mājah)

'Aqā'id

Morse Code

.-	-...	-.-.	-..	.	..-.	--.	....	..	.---
A	**B**	**C**	**D**	**E**	**F**	**G**	**H**	**I**	**J**
-.-	.-..	--	-.	---	.--.	--.-	.-.	...	-
K	**L**	**M**	**N**	**O**	**P**	**Q**	**R**	**S**	**T**
		..-	...-	.--	-..-	-.--	--..		
		U	**V**	**W**	**X**	**Y**	**Z**		

Work out the code below. / shows the end of a letter.

'Aqā'id

--- / -. / ./   --- / ..-. /   -. / .... / ./

-- / .- / .--- / --- / .-/   ... / .. / --. / -. / .../

--- / ..-. /   -. / .... / ./   -.. / .- / --.-/   --- / ..-. /

--- / ..- / -.. / --. / ./ -- / ./ -. / -/   .-- / .. / .-.. / .-../

.... / ./   -. / .... / ./   ./ -- / ./ .- / --. / ./ -. / -.-. / ./

--- / ..-. /   .- /   -... / ./ .- / .../ -/   ..-. / .- / --- / --/

-/ .... / ./   ./ .- / .- / -. / .... /

One of the major signs

The Beast

Answer the questions below:

Where will the Beast emerge from?

_____

What is one of the major signs of the Day of Judgement?

_____

The Beast will come with two things, what are these?

_____

What word will the believers be stamped with?

_____

What word will the disbelievers be stamped with?

_____

After which event will the Beast appear?

_____

Rising of the Sun from the West

Draw a poster describing the rising of the sun from the West and the Smoke.

Landslides

Find the following words in the word search:

Landslide
Three
East
West
Arabia
Fire
Yemen
Qiyāmah
Muslims
Signs
Wind
Die

Landslides

```
G X Z I Y T L D C N H F Y G I
O N L M F K Q D T M H Q E O O
E T E P Z L J S W M A E M S N
M K S D K R V L O P M D E M U
J U U E I F J F L P A B N P H
T A U V W L T Y D Q Y X W E K
E Q O K Y E S H E J I Y P T P
D I E R O R V D R R Q T S A E
V I D E C I C A N E A O D Y S
M U X K D F W K Y A E A H M S
O S P N S S E N R F L M I E L
I K I I K O L A Z T O L U L J
Z W G Z Q J B R K D S B W H H
N N G D W K X M Z U V N H I B
S L X E K R N S M A R A B I A
```

Destruction of the Ka'bah

Complete the following sentences by putting a line between the correct boxes.

'Aqā'id

The Ka'bah is the building structure in Makkah

Near the Day of Judgement, a day will come

Only the wicked and evil

They will wish to destroy the Ka'bah and

Dhu'l-Suwayqatayn from Abyssinia will

Dhu'l-Suwayqatayn is bald headed

Dhu'l-Suwayqatayn will strike the Ka'bah

Destruction of the Ka'bah

they will march to Makkah in order to destroy it.

destroy the Ka'bah and steal its treasure and Kiswah.

and has a distortion in his wrists.

with his spade and pick-axe.

shall remain in the world.

to which all the Muslims face five times a day in their ṣalāh.

when there shall be no Muslims left in the world.

Qiyāmah

Work out the answers for the following riddles.

'Aqā'id

I make a sound.
I indicate an important time.
I make a terrible noise.
What am I? _____

I will rise and blow the trumpet.
The world will be created again.
Who am I? _____

Deeds will be presented in writing.
Account will be taken.
What am I? _____

Qiyāmah

The deeds, good and bad will be weighed.
I will be used even if to measure a mustard seed.
I am a _____

"He will be the chief of all the people on the Day
of Resurrection".
Who is he? _____

Do not look into me as I am too strong to bear.
I will be bright and near on that day
What am I? _____

Qiyāmah

When the people ask Ādam عليه السلام to intercede, what will he say?

_____

_____

_____

When the people approach Nūḥ عليه السلام to intercede, what will he say?

_____

_____

_____

When the people go to Ibrāhīm عليه السلام to intercede, what will he say?

_____

_____

_____

Qiyāmah

Who will the people finally go to and ask to intercede and what will his response be?

_____

_____

_____

_____

'Aqā'id

Write a du'ā' that you will make for this time and try to recite as much Durūd as possible for the next 10 minutes.

Akhlāq

أخلاق

Trust

The words below have been taken from your coursebook. Find the words and write the sentence they appear in. Underline the word after you have completed the sentence.

Eg: 'insecure'

'Trust is a very important aspect in our lives. If there is no trust between people, they will begin to feel <u>insecure</u> and unsafe.'

'Owners' _____

'Cave' _____

'Boulder' _____

'Entrance' _____

'Pleasure' _____

'Right' _____

'Qualities' _____

'Advice' _____

'Entrusted' _____

'Corruption and hatred' _____

Akhlāq

Trust

From the story of the three men, what was the special action through which the third person asked Allāh for the large boulder to be moved?

Man Number 3: _____

_____

_____

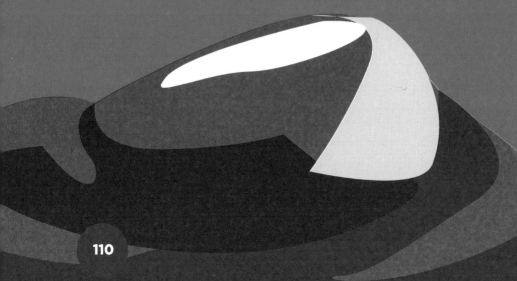

Seeking Permission

Answer the following questions.

What must you seek before entering anyone's house?

_____

What do you do if there is no one to give you permission to enter?

_____

Why is it important to seek permission before entering somebody else's house?

_____

Talk with a partner about what can happen if you both enter someone's house without seeking permission.
Make some notes below.

_____

_____

_____

Akhlāq

Seeking Permission

Put a tick in the box if the statement is true.

a. If we hear people talking in their homes we are allowed to stop and listen to their conversation.	
b. On the Day of Resurrection molten lead will be poured into the ears of those who listen to other people's private talk.	
c. Allāh سبحانه وتعالى will ask us about other people's personal lives that have nothing to do with us.	
d. We must not interfere in someone else's conversation.	
e. The Messenger صلى الله عليه وسلم said, "from the beauty of a person's Islām is to leave those things which do not concern them."	

Seeking Permission

Role Play: Work in groups of three. One can be the visitor and the other two are the hosts. Act out the situation where a visitor enters without permission. Change roles then act out the situation when a visitor enters with permission and discuss the difference. Write down the results below:

_____

_____

_____

_____

_____

_____

_____

_____

_____

Seeking Permission

Design a poster with key points from the chapter of asking permission before entering

Moving Harm from the Road

Choose one ḥadīth from the pages of this topic and draw a descriptive picture relating to it below.

Moving Harm from the Road

Over the next week aim to move at least 5 different things from the street that could cause harm. Record what it is and what you did in the table below.

Date	Type of harmful object	What I did

Moving Harm from the Road

Answer the following questions:

What is a simple act that we can be rewarded for?

_____

What action did the man perform that is loved by Allāh سبحانه وتعالى and what was the reward for it?

_____

What sort of person does Allāh سبحانه وتعالى detest?

_____

Why should you remove harmful objects from the road?

_____

Summarise the ḥadīth of Abū Barza رضي الله عنه below.

_____

_____

_____

_____

Akhlāq

Moving Harm from the Road

In the columns below, write out things which you think are good and bad relating to the road.

Good	Bad

Akhlāq

Moving Harm from the Road

Draw a picture below of a road with at least 5 harmful objects and label them.

Now draw a picture of a road with no harmful objects.

Being a Good Neighbour

Colour the ḥadīth below about neighbours.

"He is not a believer, he who eats to his fill, whilst his neighbour besides him goes hungry."

Being a Good Neighbour

List 10 things you can do to be a good neighbour

1._____

2._____

3._____

4._____

5._____

6._____

7._____

8._____

9_____

10._____

Akhlāq

Being a Good Neighbour

Fill in the blanks

"Worship Allāh سبحانه وتعالى, and do not _____ anything with Him, and be good to _____ and to kinsmen and _____ and the needy and the close neighbour and the _____ neighbour and the companion at your side and the _____ and to those (slaves who are) owned by you. Surely, Allāh سبحانه وتعالى does not like those who are _____, proud." (Qur'ān 4:36)

The Messenger of Allāh صلى الله عليه وسلم observed: "He will not enter _____ when his neighbour is not _____ from his wrongful conduct."
(Ṣaḥīḥ Muslim)

Being a Good Neighbour

Work with a partner to find the following verses from the Qu'rān.

Write the name of the sūrah they are in and try reciting them in Arabic.

When My servants ask you about Me, then (tell them that) I am near. I respond to the call of one when he prays to Me; so they should respond to Me, and have faith in Me, so that they may be on the right path. (Qur'ān 2:186)

Sūrah name:

Your Lord has said, "Call Me, I will respond to you (Qur'ān 40:60)

Sūrah name:

Or the one who responds to a helpless person when He prays to Him and removes distress (Qur'ān 27:62)

Sūrah name:

Akhlāq

123

Ādāb

آداب

Ādāb of Du'ā'

Write down the some of etiquettes of making du'ā'.

1._____

2._____

3._____

4._____

5._____

6_____

7._____

8._____

9_____

10._____

Work with a partner and see if you can memorise the following du'ā' in Arabic.

"Our Lord, give us good in this world and good in the Hereafter, and save us from the punishment of Fire." (Qur'ān 2:201)

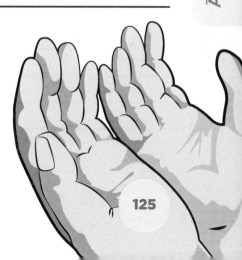

125

Ādāb of Du'ā'

Compare these two du'ā's. Which one is the better way of asking from Allāh سبحانه وتعالى? Explain why one of them is a good way of asking and the other is not.

> O Allāh, you are the Greatest, the One who is Most Merciful. O Allāh, send mercy and blessings on the Best of Mankind. Please forgive my mistakes and give me goodness and help me in everything thing I do. O Allāh, I need new shoes, please make it possible for me to buy some...

_____
_____
_____
_____

> O Allah, I want new shoes. Can you give me new shoes? I really want them before my next holidays.

_____
_____
_____

Ādāb of Dressing

Work in a group with four people. One person will be the teacher, the other three will be students who ask many questions regarding what is being taught. The teacher will explain the ādāb of dressing to the students. In your groups you may change roles so each of you has a chance to play the teacher role.

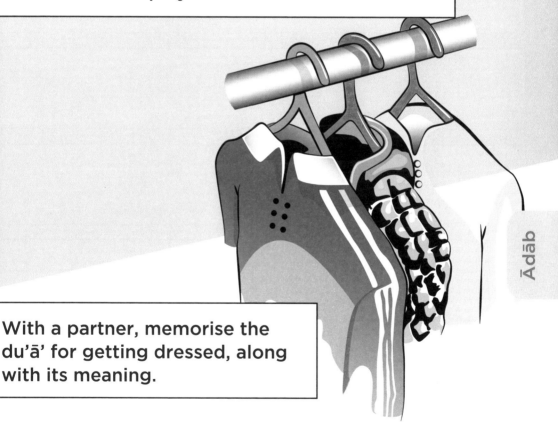

With a partner, memorise the du'ā' for getting dressed, along with its meaning.

Ādāb of Guests & Hosts

After reading through the ādāb of guests and hosts, create 5 questions which have a one or two word answer. The answer cannot be a 'yes' or 'no'.

Example: What was the good news that the angels gave to Ibrāhīm عليه السلام?
Answer: Knowledgeable boy

Ādāb of Guests & Hosts

Imagine you are having a guest visit you. Think of your guest as a friend from your class. Write 10 DO's and DON'T's of the ādāb of a host. Use the information from your coursebook and also write some points of your own.

DO's	DON'T's
1	1
2	2
3	3
4	4
5	5
6	6
7	7
8	8
9	9
10	10

Ādāb of a Gathering

After reading through the ādāb of gathering, create 5 questions, then get the person sitting next to you to answer them.

Ādāb of a Gathering

Create a poster about how you should behave in a gathering

Ādāb of Istinjā'

Work in groups of four and discuss the etiquettes of Istinjā'.

Answer 'True' or 'False' for the statements below:

"People should fear being cursed for two things; like those who urinate and excrete in the roads where people walk, and in the shades of people" (like trees which they may use to have a picnic).

_____

Someone had been punished in the grave because he didn't prevent urine from falling on him, and as for the other he used to cause problems amongst people.

_____

Enter with your right foot.

_____

Cover your hair.

_____

We don't have to recite the du'ā'.

_____

Wash your hands before placing them inside a bucket or container

_____

Lower the body as much as possible before removing any garments.

_____

Ādāb

Ādāb of Istinjā'

Make sure your front or back is facing the Qiblah.

Talk a lot.

Do not urinate whilst standing.

You can call your friend and have a phone conversation.

Use tissue paper followed by water to ensure cleanliness.

Wipe and wash yourself with the right hand.

Wait a little while to ensure all the drops have come out.

Leave with right foot.

Recite the du'ā' when leaving

Ādāb